HOW TO BE A FOOTBALLER
AND OTHER SPORTS JOBS

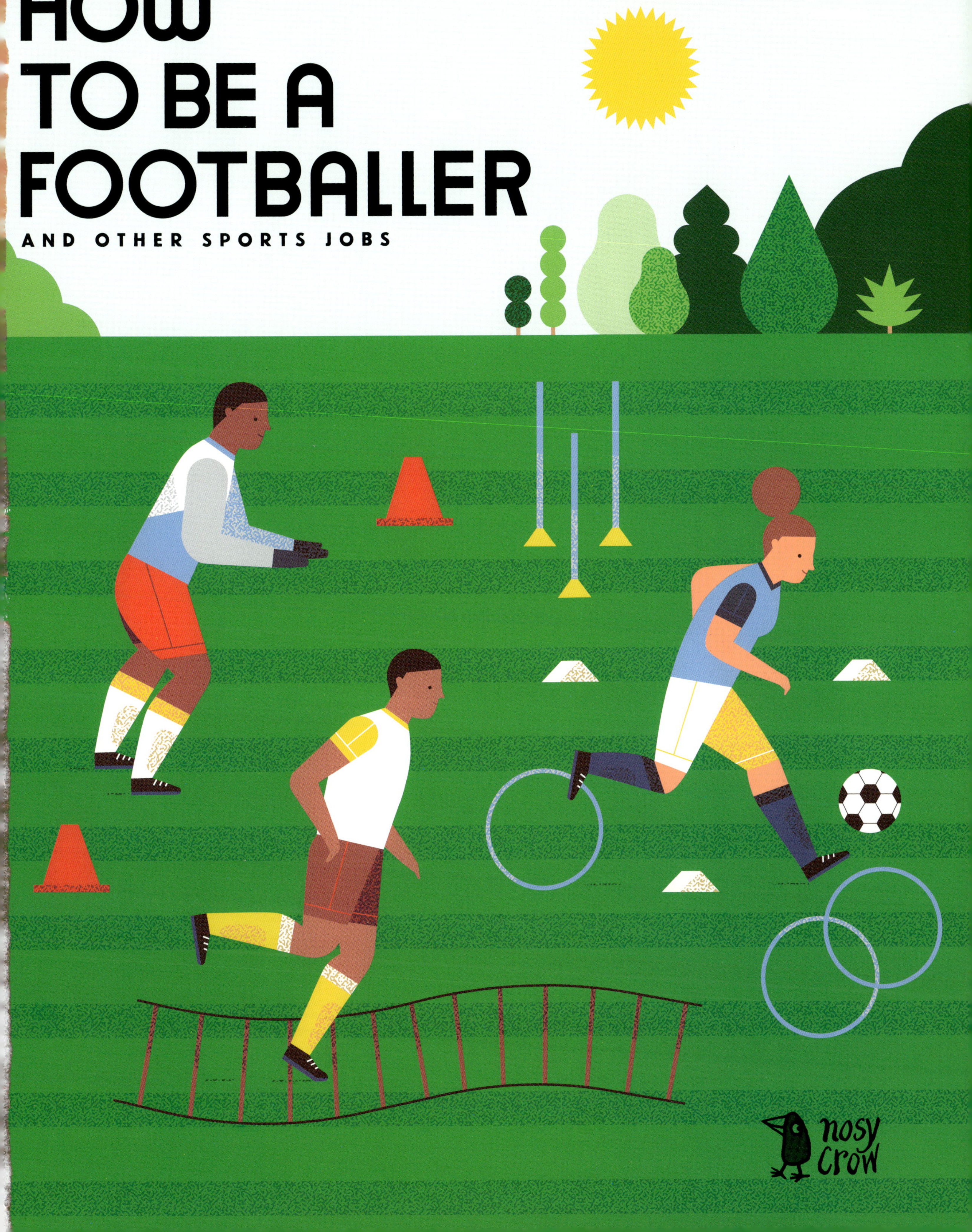

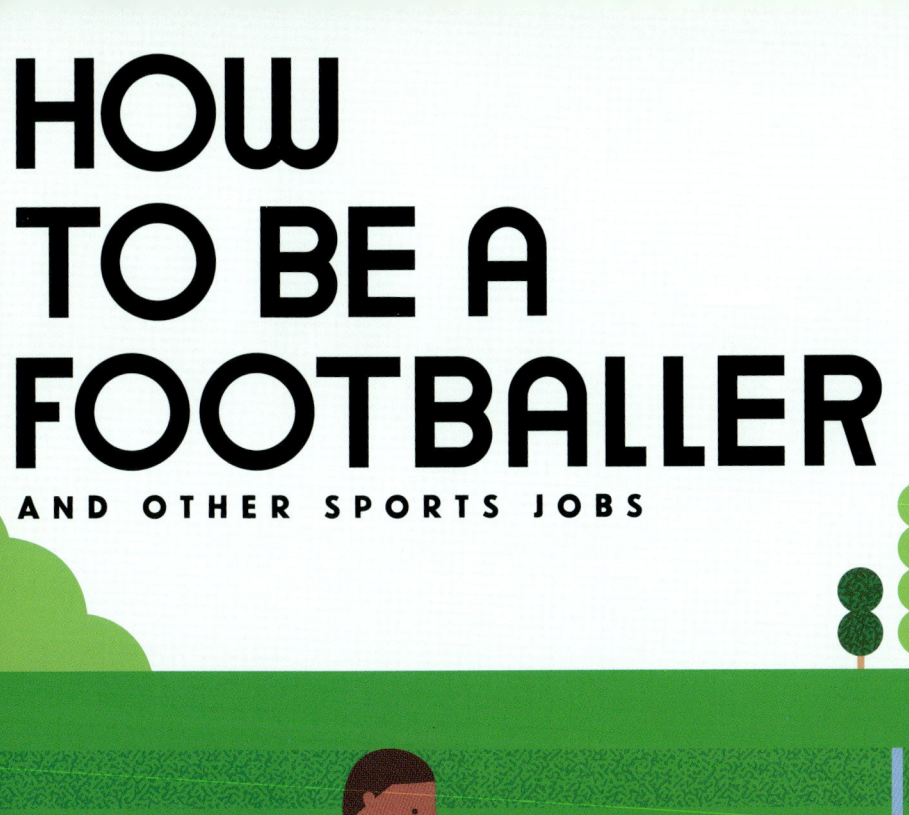

nosy crow

To all the girls and boys who love football . . .

I hope this book can show you that football is a game for everyone. Enjoy! With special dedication to Jeyla, Aaron, Lucia, Amari and Lara – dream big little ones x
R.Y.

. . . especially a little one named Manu.
S.L.

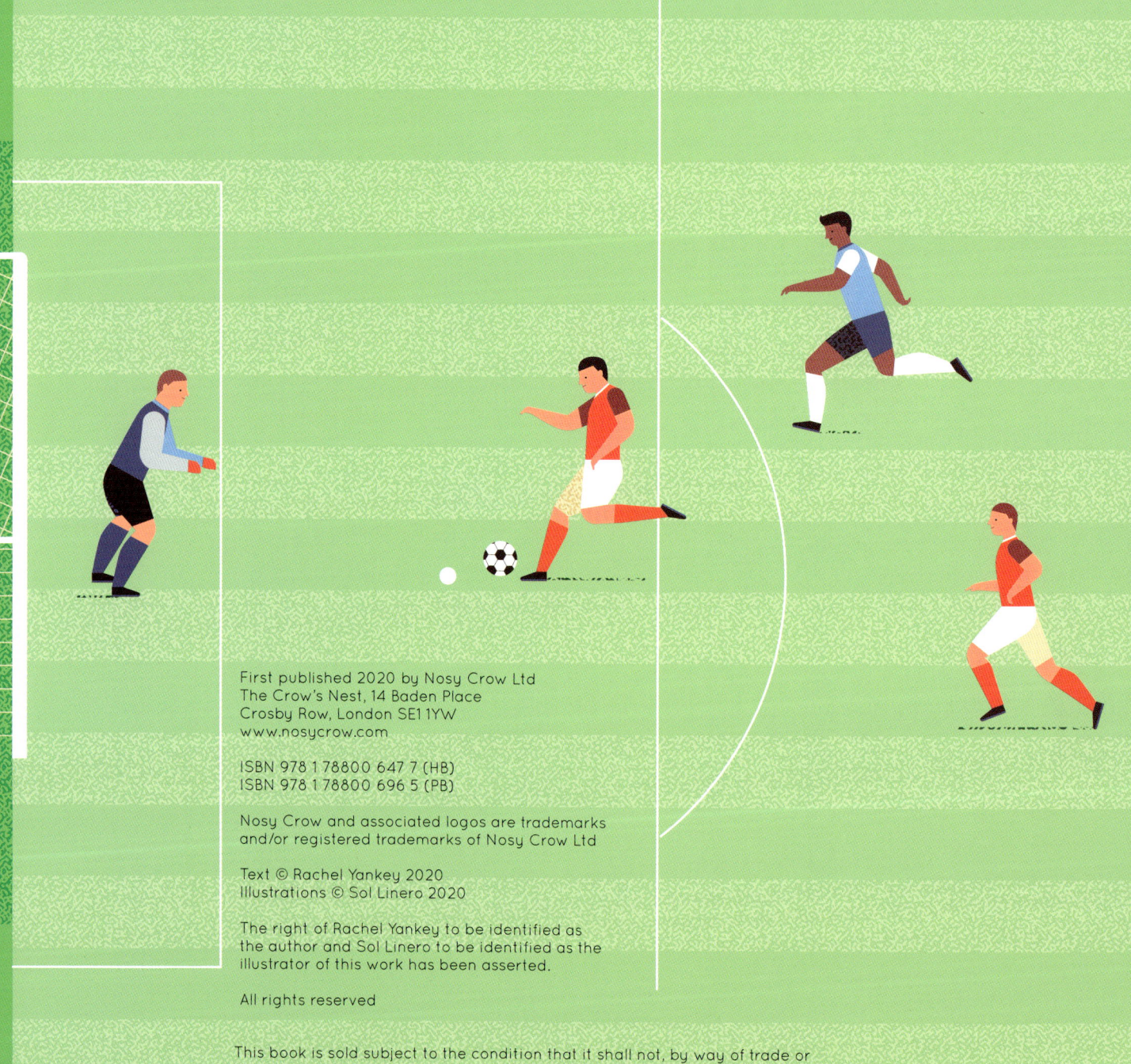

First published 2020 by Nosy Crow Ltd
The Crow's Nest, 14 Baden Place
Crosby Row, London SE1 1YW
www.nosycrow.com

ISBN 978 1 78800 647 7 (HB)
ISBN 978 1 78800 696 5 (PB)

Nosy Crow and associated logos are trademarks and/or registered trademarks of Nosy Crow Ltd

Text © Rachel Yankey 2020
Illustrations © Sol Linero 2020

The right of Rachel Yankey to be identified as the author and Sol Linero to be identified as the illustrator of this work has been asserted.

All rights reserved

This book is sold subject to the condition that it shall not, by way of trade or otherwise, be lent, hired out or otherwise circulated in any form of binding or cover other than that in which it is published. No part of this publication may be reproduced, stored in a retrieval system, or transmitted in any form or by any means (electronic, mechanical, photocopying, recording or otherwise) without the prior written permission of Nosy Crow Ltd.

Nosy Crow does not have control over, or any responsibility for, any author or third-party websites referred to in or on this book.

A CIP catalogue record for this book is available from the British Library.

Printed in China

Papers used by Nosy Crow are made from wood grown in sustainable forests.

10 9 8 7 6 5 4 3 2 1 (HB)
10 9 8 7 6 5 4 3 2 1 (PB)

CONTENTS

WHAT IS FOOTBALL?	4
THE HISTORY OF FOOTBALL	6
WHY PLAY FOOTBALL?	9
PLAYING FOOTBALL TODAY	10
WHAT ARE THE RULES OF FOOTBALL?	12
HOW DO YOU BECOME A FOOTBALLER?	14
WHAT KIND OF TRAINING DO FOOTBALLERS HAVE TO DO?	16
HOW DO YOU PREPARE FOR A FOOTBALL MATCH?	18
WHAT DOES EACH PERSON DO IN A FOOTBALL TEAM?	20
WHAT DO FOOTBALLERS DO WHEN THEY'RE NOT PLAYING?	22
WHAT OTHER JOBS ARE THERE ON THE PITCH?	24
WHAT OTHER KINDS OF FOOTBALL JOBS ARE THERE?	26
WHAT ABOUT A JOB IN FOOTBALL MEDIA?	28
ARE THERE ANY MORE UNUSUAL FOOTBALL JOBS?	30
GET INVOLVED!	32

WHAT IS FOOTBALL?

Football is the most popular sport in the world. It is watched and loved in more or less every country and it can be played anywhere by anyone. But what actually is it?

Football is a fast, active team sport played between **two teams of 11 players.** Each team runs around a pitch – kicking, tackling and scoring goals. Because you don't need much equipment – **all you need is some space and a ball** – and you can play with smaller teams if you like, it's an easy sport to start.

Lots of people enjoy playing football for fun, but some people are so talented, **football has become their job.** This is known as playing professionally and these footballers actually get **paid to play the world's favourite game.**

Most countries have hundreds of **football clubs** based in towns or cities with teams that play at different levels. At each level, the teams compete in a **league system** – a competition where teams play each other across a season to see who will be crowned the champion.

Not all leagues are made up of professional players, but the leagues at the highest levels usually are. These contain between 10–24 teams and a season of games can last up to 10 months. The top leagues, such as the Premier League in the UK, are watched by millions.

DID YOU KNOW?
In the USA, football has been called 'soccer' since the 1800s. It comes from the SOC in Football AsSOCiation.

THE HISTORY OF FOOTBALL

Ball games have been played all over the world for thousands of years, but where did the game of football as we know it begin?

Ancient Chinese soldiers played *tsu chu*. The players had to kick a ball through a hole in a cloth tied to two posts.

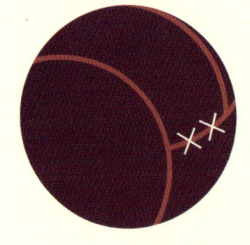

European villagers played ball games against each other in the streets.

The first football club in the world, Sheffield FC, was formed in England.

200 BC   100 BC   1200-1300   1848   1857

Ancient Greeks introduced ball games at the Olympics.

The 'Cambridge Rules' were introduced in England. They allowed throw-ins and goal kicks and disallowed running while holding the ball.

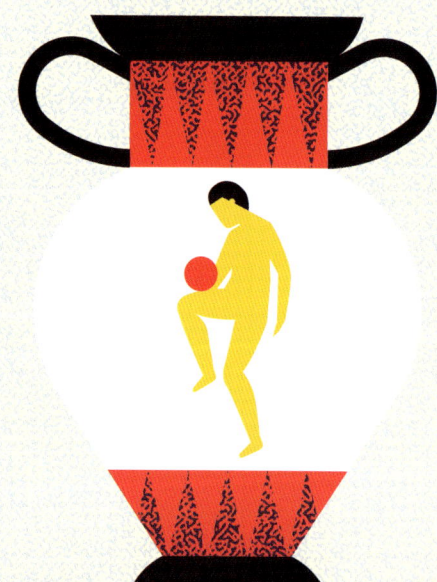

1863 — The Football Association (FA) was formed in the UK (Scottish FA was formed in 1873), and fouling was banned.

1888 — The English Football League was founded and three years later goal nets were introduced so players could tell if they had scored.

1904 — FIFA was formed. This is the organisation that looks after football tournaments worldwide.

1921 — Women's football was very popular during the First World War. Lily Parr was one of the first female footballers and her team, Dick Kerr's Ladies, were the first to wear shorts and play games in different countries. A few years later, the FA decided to ban women's football. They were worried that people would be less interested in the men's game if women's football became too popular.

1930 — The first World Cup kicked off in Uruguay, South America – and Uruguay won! The trophy was named after the man who invented the competition, Jules Rimet.

England won the World Cup, 4–2 in a match against Germany. It was held in England and the final was at the old Wembley stadium. The World Cup trophy was stolen and found one week later by a dog named Pickles.

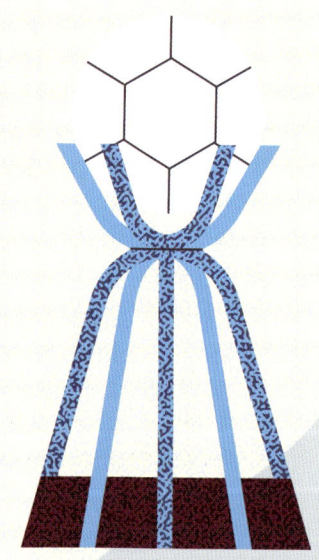

The first Women's World Cup kicked off in China and was won by the USA.

Fulham Ladies Football Club became the first full-time professional women's club in England.

Over one billion people tuned in to watch France beat Croatia 4–2 in the World Cup final in Russia.

1966   1969   1991   2000   2012   2018

The Women's Football Association (WFA) was formed in England and two years later the FA lifted the ban on women's football.

At the World Cup in Japan, automatic goal line technology was first used to decide whether the ball has crossed the line or not. Because it's very expensive, it is only used for games at the highest level today.

WHY PLAY FOOTBALL?

Playing football is a great way to make friends and keep fit, but it's also an exciting sport to follow.

From **superstar professionals** to friends playing in the street, everyone enjoys watching a fast-paced, action-packed game. If you support a team, whether they are local or far away, every game is an opportunity to see some **incredible goals** and spectacular player skills.

In order to enjoy watching football, we need people who work in the 'football industry'. Jobs vary from . . .

managers   and doctors,   to referees   and journalists.

And, of course . . . footballers!

PLAYING FOOTBALL TODAY

Today, the best professional footballers get to play in tournaments all over the world.

The World Cup is one of the biggest tournaments in sport. It is played every four years and hosted by a different country each time. Over 100 countries enter the competition, and 32 teams get through to the final stage for the men's World Cup and 24 teams for the women's. They play matches over four weeks until eventually one country is crowned **World Champions**.

DID YOU KNOW?
Brazil have won the World Cup the most times – five! The USA have won the Women's World Cup three times.

The Confederations Cup is a competition between the current World Champions, the hosts of the next World Cup and the six champions of the continental championships. It is great practice for the World Cup and held every four years.

The Olympics has included football since 1900 and women's football since 1996. To make it different from the World Cup, only players that are under 23 years old are allowed to play. However, three over-age players can play in the men's team and there is no age limit for women.

CONCACAF GOLD CUP

UEFA CHAMPION'S LEAGUE

AFC ASIAN CUP

CAF AFRICAN CUP OF NATIONS

CONMEBOL COPA AMERICA

OFC NATION'S CUP

There are **six continental championships** for national teams from each continent. These are played every two to four years: the Asian Cup, European Championships, Copa America, African Cup of Nations, Gold Cup and OFC Nations Cup.

Paralympic football includes versions of the game with different rules and equipment for players with impairments. Blind football is played on a smaller pitch with fewer players. The ball has a rattle inside, so the players can find it by listening out for the sound.

WHAT ARE THE RULES OF FOOTBALL?

Football is played on a football pitch. This is a rectangular area, split into two halves with the same line markings on each side.

Penalty spot – if a foul is committed by the defending team in the area around the goal, the attacking team gets a penalty. They place the ball on the penalty spot and try to get it past the goalkeeper with just one kick.

Goal line – if the whole ball crosses this line between the goal posts, a goal is awarded to the attacking team.

"Drop!" Move back towards your own goal.

"Switch it!" Pass the ball to the other side of the pitch.

"Player on!" Watch out for the player that's about to tackle you.

DID YOU KNOW? When a player scores three goals in a match, it is known as a hat-trick.

A game lasts for **90 minutes** – 45 minutes in each half with a short break in between. Teams attack one goal during the first half, then switch ends and attack the other goal in the second half.

Like every sport, football has many **rules to learn**. If the referee shows you a **red card**, you have been sent off and must leave the pitch immediately. A **yellow card** is shown as a warning if you foul, dive or argue with the referee. If you are shown two yellow cards in the same game, this equals a red card.

"Push up!" Move up the pitch to get closer to the ball.

A foul is when a player does something in a match that the referee thinks is against the rules of the game.

Centre spot – the ball is placed here to start the game at the beginning, after half time and after a goal is scored.

Diving is when a player pretends to be injured to make it look like a player on the other team has fouled.

HOW DO YOU BECOME A FOOTBALLER?

Playing football at the highest level is hard physical work, so first of all you need to be incredibly fit and healthy. Some players run as far as 15 kilometres per game!

To understand **how to play,** you can start off by watching football matches and copying what you see players do on the pitch. If you have fun trying to learn these skills and enjoy working in a team, you could join a team at your school or locally.

Here, you'll need to **listen to your coach** and **practise as much as you can**, on your own or with your friends. The more you practise the easier it gets – especially if you practise playing using both feet. Your coach will **develop your confidence** and help you to become brave and good on the ball. You'll need to recover quickly if you've had a bad game, so it's important not to get too upset if you lose.

Football academies are special boarding schools with training schemes to **develop talented young players.** In an academy, players would train every day and have normal school lessons too. To get into an academy, you need to sign up for a trial or be scouted by a **talent scout**.

Football trials are where coaches test the players' technique and how calm they are under pressure. The coach or scout will be looking for players that stand out to earn a spot on a youth team.

A lot of teams do fitness testing to measure the strength, speed and power of their players. This means the coaches can create a **special training programme** for each player.

Every player is different and depending on the position they play in, they will be required to do a **different job** on the pitch.

WHAT KIND OF TRAINING DO FOOTBALLERS HAVE TO DO?

Footballers play a match about once a week and the rest of their time is spent getting ready to play by training for around two to four hours a day.

On a normal training day, footballers arrive at the training ground early in the morning. They always need to pay special attention to what they eat, so for breakfast, footballers will eat something healthy, with enough **carbohydrate and protein** to give them energy.

After breakfast, it's time for a **team meeting** to talk about what each player is going to be focusing on that day.

Then the players will start training to **improve their ball skills and teamwork**. This is usually made up of various exercises done over and over again, known as **drills**.

All footballers start with the most basic skill of all – **how to kick the ball**. Footballers never use their toes as they could get injured easily. Instead, they use their 'instep' which is where the laces are on their football boots. This gives the kick **power, control and height**.

Once footballers have mastered basic kicking, they will work on drills to improve the more complicated skills needed in a match . . .

passing,

shooting,

tackling,

heading,

Remember to keep your head up and look where you're going when you're dribbling!

dribbling,

and saving.

HOW DO YOU PREPARE FOR A FOOTBALL MATCH?

Match days are very different from normal training days. Firstly, the match could be anywhere, so the team might need to travel to get there.

Then, all footballers apart from the goalkeeper wear the same kit: a t-shirt, shorts, socks, shin pads and football boots. **Goalkeepers wear a different colour** from their teammates and the opposition, so the referee can easily identify them. They also wear **gloves with grip** because they can use their hands to pick up the ball.

A team normally has a **favourite colour** that they play in called the **'home' kit**. So they never clash with the opposition, they will have a second kit in a **different colour** called the **'away' kit**. Some teams have a third kit which is a different colour again. In 1933, footballers started wearing **numbers and their surnames on their shirts**, so referees could tell them apart.

Before a game, the players need to **warm up**. A warm up is a series of football actions, like running and kicking, that start off slowly and get faster and faster. This means the heart pumps more blood to the muscles to make them soft, stretchy and ready for action. It's also a good way to prevent injury and get your mind ready to play.

DID YOU KNOW?
Before teams had matching kits, they wore matching hats. Nowadays, players don't wear hats, but every time they play an international game for their country, they are said to be 'capped'.

The team manager will then talk to the team about **tactics** for the game ahead. These are special moves, positions and ideas that the players can use during the match and they're different every game depending on the team being played.

Before an international match, both teams sing their **national anthem** – the away team first and then the home team. It's also played at major events like the FA Cup Final.

WHAT DOES EACH PERSON DO IN A
FOOTBALL TEAM?

Footballers need different skills to play in each position on a team.

Some players are **adaptable** which means they can play in **more than one position**. To play well together, the 10 outfield players and goalkeeper all need to **communicate** and **listen** to instructions from the manager.

Goalkeepers are the only players that have the whole game being played in front of them, so they need to be good at telling the team where they should be on the pitch. They should **be brave** and **quick** to react to shots. Goalkeepers are **often very tall** and it helps if they have **big hands** as well!

Defenders need to be able to **spot danger** and try to prevent the opposition from attacking and scoring. They need to be good at **heading the ball** and paying attention to the game.

Every team has a **captain**. The captain needs to be a **strong leader** with a **positive attitude**. They should be kind and helpful to the rest of their team and be excellent at giving instructions and **listening to others**.

DID YOU KNOW?
The captain usually wears an armband so everyone knows who they are.

Attackers need good awareness and **fast movement** in front of the goal. They need to take responsibility for shooting, be calm, have quick-thinking and **not be afraid to miss**.

Midfielders need to be able to attack and defend for the team. They should be **good all-rounders** with plenty of stamina, or energy, to run up and down the pitch, and they should be **good at tackling** and passing the ball.

WHAT DO FOOTBALLERS DO WHEN THEY'RE NOT PLAYING?

Very few footballers get to play professional football full-time. Semi-professional players will probably have another job outside of football. This could be anything at all – from chefs to carpenters!

Footballers don't stay in the same team forever. In fact, they are **bought and sold** by different clubs all the time, during periods called **'transfer windows'** – one in the summer and one in the winter. This means they need to be good at settling in and making friends quickly.

Sometimes players move to a team in a different country where they might not even speak the language. When this happens, language lessons are extremely useful, but they also find that **playing football as a team** is a brilliant way to get to know each other.

DID YOU KNOW?
Footballers also might do interviews, meet the public and do advertising work with commercial brands, so you have to be good at talking to people.

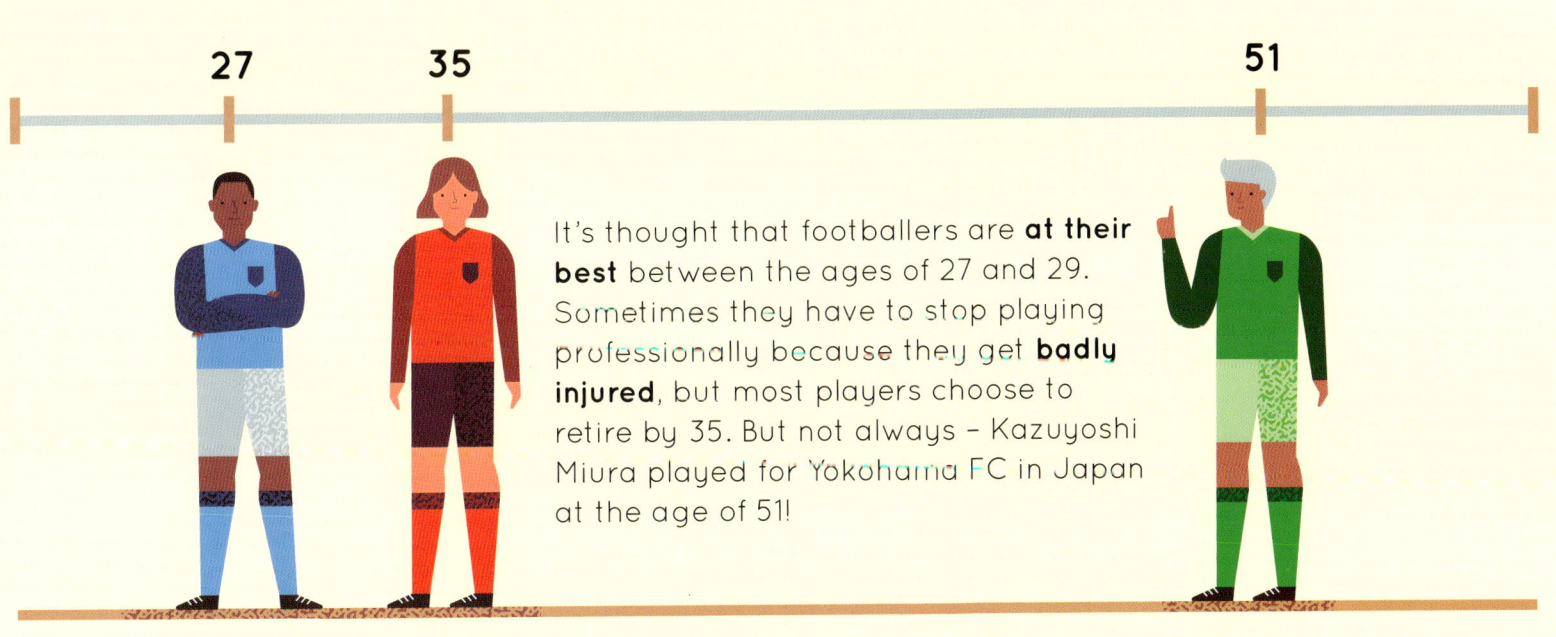

It's thought that footballers are **at their best** between the ages of 27 and 29. Sometimes they have to stop playing professionally because they get **badly injured**, but most players choose to retire by 35. But not always – Kazuyoshi Miura played for Yokohama FC in Japan at the age of 51!

When footballers **aren't in training** or playing matches, or even if they're retired, they still keep busy!

Many play **other sports** where you are less likely to get hurt, like golf, swimming or fishing.

Some even practise yoga or ballet to increase their **flexibility**, **strength** and **balance**.

Like everyone, they also have **hobbies that they enjoy** like playing online games, reading and listening to music.

WHAT OTHER JOBS ARE THERE ON THE PITCH?

Are you good at sticking to the rules? Then a job running the game might be for you. There are many experts working in football whose job it is to make sure matches run smoothly.

There are two **assistant referees** who run up and down the touchline and use flags to signal to the referee. They notice details of the game that the referee might not be able to see.

There is always a **referee** in charge to keep track of time and make sure the **match is played fairly**. They need to be good at making quick decisions about what is **right and wrong** and not be scared of the crowd who might 'boo' if they don't agree with a decision.

Football teams usually employ a **groundskeeper** to take care of the pitch. They **look after the grass** in all kinds of weather all year round to make sure it doesn't freeze over or dry out.

BOX OFFICE

There are many different jobs that need to be carried out so a **stadium is ready** for a game, such as **ticketing staff** to sell tickets.

There are also **people selling food and drink**, **stewards** to help keep fans safe and help with directions, **cleaners** to keep the stadium tidy and many more.

WHAT OTHER KINDS OF FOOTBALL JOBS ARE THERE?

For every footballer that gets to play in front of thousands of fans, there are hundreds of people working hard to get them there. But what do these people actually do?

Each team has a club **doctor** who will take care of every player. They will also be on the side of the pitch on match days **in case of any unexpected injuries**. This job is very important as players often bash into each other during matches, so the risk of injury is very high.

A football agent works for the player or manager to advise them about the **best opportunities** for their career. They handle contracts and negotiate deals before a player joins a club or works with any commercial brands.

The **football manager** is responsible for **picking the team**, and deciding on tactics and training. They make sure the players feel prepared and confident, buy and sell new players and speak to the media. A good manager should understand what each player does best and help everyone **work well together** within the team.

If a player gets injured during a match, a **physiotherapist** (also known as a **physio**) will come on to the pitch to check whether they are OK. If it is only a minor injury, they will use a **'magic spray'** to numb the injured area so the player can carry on.

Working with the manager, the **team coach** is in charge of **training the team**. There is normally more than one coach for the players and a separate one for the goalkeepers. Often coaches have played football themselves in the past.

WHAT ABOUT A JOB IN
FOOTBALL MEDIA?

There are all kinds of media jobs in the industry, from retired footballers who have become 'pundits' to give their expert opinions on television, to people behind the scenes making sure fans can follow all the matches.

A **commentator** will **report to the viewers** exactly what's happening, moment by moment, during the game. Commentators work very closely with the television or radio production team, such as sound engineers and producers.

A **journalist** writes articles about how a team has played, individual players, and any **interesting news stories**. These can be printed in newspapers, magazines or read online.

A **press officer** is in charge of arranging any interviews for the players. They are also responsible for the **weekly press conference** for the manager before and after the game. This is where journalists get to ask managers and players questions.

ARE THERE ANY MORE UNUSUAL FOOTBALL JOBS?

Most **talent scouts** work for football clubs to find talented players to join their team. There are different types of scouts who work in different age groups of football, such as under 16, under 18 and under 21. They have to **travel a lot**, so you'll need to enjoy life on the road.

DID YOU KNOW?
Some players, such as Lionel Messi of Barcelona FC earn over $100 million a year!

A **sports lawyer** normally takes care of any legal work that players might need. They are often in charge of writing up long, complicated contracts so you'll need to have **patience** and an **excellent eye for detail**.

Some teams have a **team chef** who prepares all the food for the players at the training ground and before and after every match.

A **photographer** will work with the team to take lots of pictures that can be used in programmes, on **social media**, inside the club shop and many other places to **advertise the club**.

Football is a game for everybody so clubs have a special department to help them stay connected with other **organisations in the community**, like schools and charities. **Outreach officers** need to be good at speaking to people and making new friends.

GET INVOLVED!

If you would like to learn more about football jobs or working in the football industry, there are many things you can do . . .

To start with, all you need is a ball! You could set up your own games with some friends and if you find that you enjoy playing, you could join a football team at school or sign up to your local football club.

You can start playing football at any age and the FA have guidelines online for junior games for the under 7/8s, under 9/10s, under 11/12s, under 13/14s, under 15/16s and under 17/18s.

Useful organisations and websites include:
The Professional Footballers' Association www.thepfa.com
The Football Association www.thefa.com
The Football Association Youth Football Guide
http://www.thefa.com/get-involved/player/youth
Union of European Football Associations www.uefa.com
FIFA www.fifa.com
FIFPro (Football Players Worldwide) www.fifpro.org

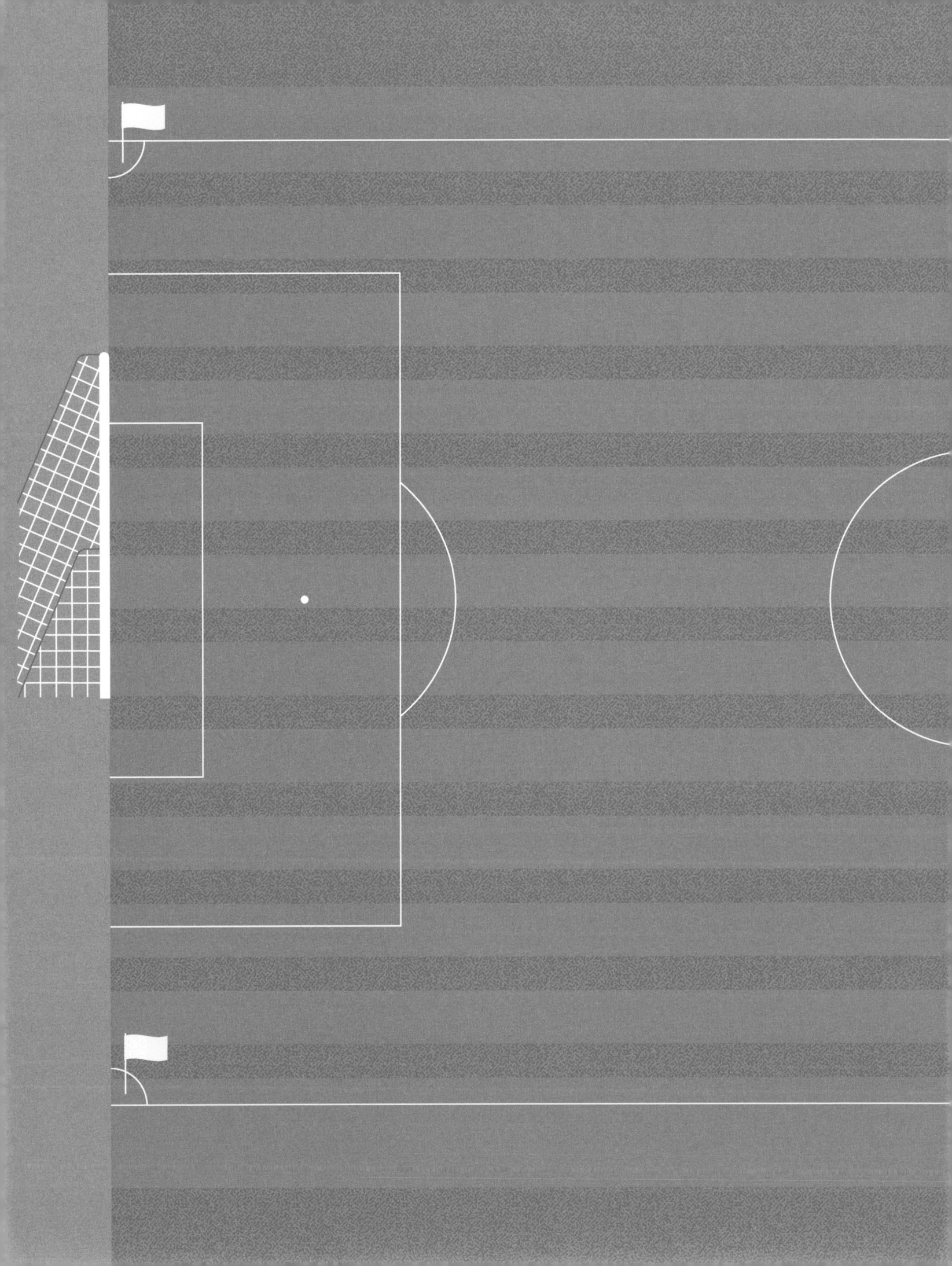